Usborne Activities

Over 80 Brain Puzzles

D0559082

Pencil match-up

Draw a circle around the two pencil pictures that can be turned so that they match each other exactly.

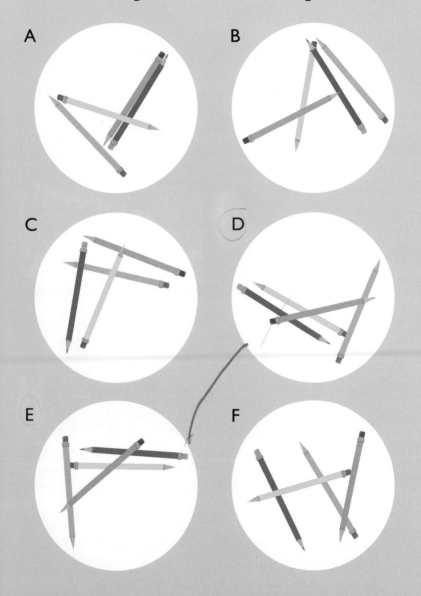

A

B

C

D

E

F

At the zoo

Study this scene for one minute, then turn the page.

At the zoo

Look at the previous page for one minute, then try to answer these questions **without looking back at the scene again**.

1. How many snakes are in the snake enclosure?

Answer: two

2. What is the man in the hat holding?

Answer: Ballons

3. What food is in the porcupine enclosure?

Answer: carrot

4. How many of the penguins are swimming?

Answer: one

5. What is the little boy holding?

Answer: ice cream

Monkey meals

These monkeys will gain a number of units of energy from each of the fruits they've collected. Use the key to calculate which pile of fruit will give the most energy.

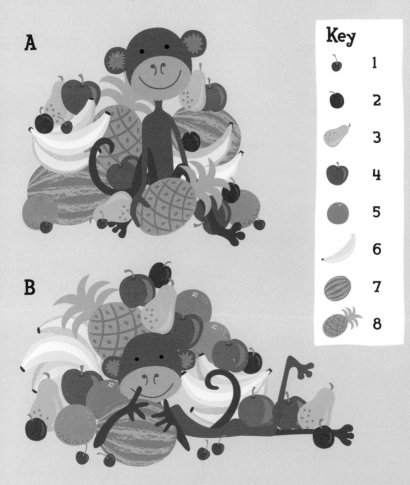

A

B

Key
1
2
3
4
5
6
7
8

Answer: ....

Bees and butterflies

Follow the trails to see which insect visited which flower.

Flitter

Bizzy

Buzzy

Flutter

Red flower: _FLUTTER_

Orange flower: _Buzzy_

Blue flower: _BIZZY_

Purple flower: _Flitter_

Picture memory

Look at these paintings for one minute, then turn the page and read the instructions below the paintings.

Picture memory

Look at the previous page to find out how to do this puzzle.

One of the paintings has been stolen. Can you draw the missing painting in the empty space?

Country search

Find the names of the countries
below in the grid and draw around
them like this:

Brazil   **Canada**   **China**

Italy   **Kenya**   **Peru**

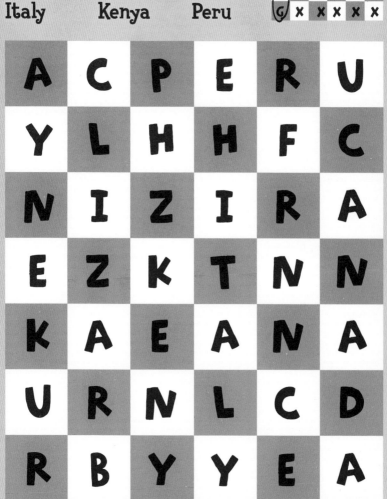

A	C	P	E	R	U
Y	L	H	H	F	C
N	I	Z	I	R	A
E	Z	K	T	N	N
K	A	E	A	N	A
U	R	N	L	C	D
R	B	Y	Y	E	A

Folding up

Which **four** of the green shapes below could fold up to make a triangular prism (shown in the middle)?

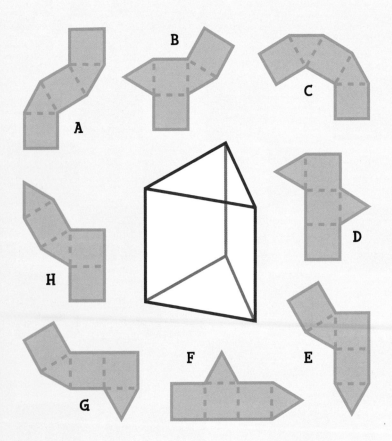

Answer: ....

Planet paths

You are a space courier and your job is to deliver packages to each of the nine planets below. Can you draw the route your rocket will take, using only four straight lines and without taking your pen off the page? You can't go back along any of the lines you've already made.

Start •

Patches

In the patchwork pattern below, draw squares around the 3x3 blocks that match the blocks shown on the right.

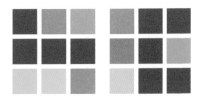

Puppy prize-giving

Alfie, Boxer, Charlie, Daisy and Elmo took part in a dog agility race. Alfie finished before Boxer, but behind Charlie. Daisy finished before Elmo, but behind Boxer. Can you draw lines to link each dog to their trophy?

On and off

John is standing outside a closed door next to three light switches. Each switch controls one of three lightbulbs behind the door. All three switches are in the Off position. He can only see the bulbs by going into the next room, but once there, he's not allowed to go back to the switches. How many switches will he have to turn on to know which switch controls which bulb?

Answer:

....

Empty pyramid

Which number should be placed in the empty pyramid?

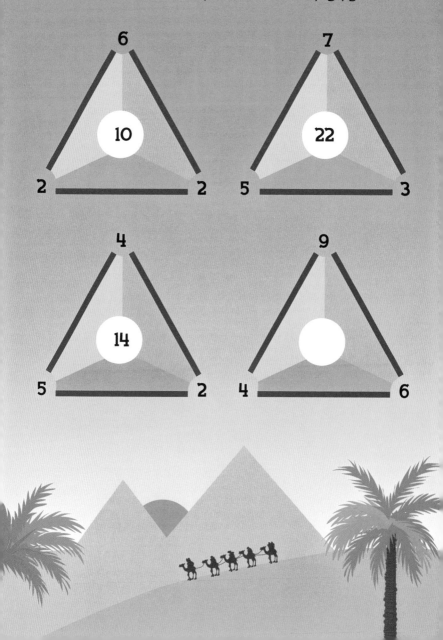

Traffic jam

Study these vehicles, then compare them with the silhouettes on the opposite page.

1

2

3

4

5

6

7

8

9

10

11

12

13

14

15

Match the silhouettes to the vehicles. Write the correct number next to each letter.

A ....

B ....

C ....

D ....

E ....

F ....

G ....

H ....

I ....

J ....

K ....

L ....

M ....

N ....

O ....

Spot the difference

Study the picture below, then compare it with the one on the right.

Circle **six** differences in this picture.

Going dotty

Shade in the shapes with dots. What can you see?

Twin chains

These chains are made up of links that are all gold, all silver, or half gold and half silver. A link shown on its side, like this, could be all gold, or half gold and half silver.

Draw rings around the two chains that could be made up of the same sequence of links.

A

B

C

D

E

Spell check

Underline the spelling mistakes in this book report.

Tommy, The Timid T-rex

This book is about a dinosuar who is afriad of evrything, even his own refletion. His dad is embarrased by him and he does'nt have any freinds because he is two boring to play with. One day, he meats a mouse who is brave, even thuogh he is little. The mouse teaches Toomy how to be brave to. I liked this book a lot becuase it was funy.

On the move

Can you think of the solutions to these riddles? Check the answer pages to see if you're correct.

Riddle 1: Trains travel from Bridgetown to Castleville all day, always on the same track, always going nonstop and at the same speed. The noon train took 80 minutes to complete the trip, but the 4pm train took an hour and 20 minutes. Can you explain how this is possible?

Riddle 2: I'm not a bird, but I can fly through the sky. I'm not a river, but I'm full of water. What am I?

Riddle 3: How could a cowboy ride into a town on Friday, stay two days, and then ride out on Friday?

Riddle 4: A black dog is sleeping in the middle of a black road. There are no streetlights and no moonlight. A car comes speeding down the road with its lights off and its stereo blasting. As it gets close to the dog, it slows down and safely steers around it. How did the driver know the dog was there?

Statues

Study these statues, then compare them with the ones on the opposite page.

1

2

3

4

Circle the same four statues here.

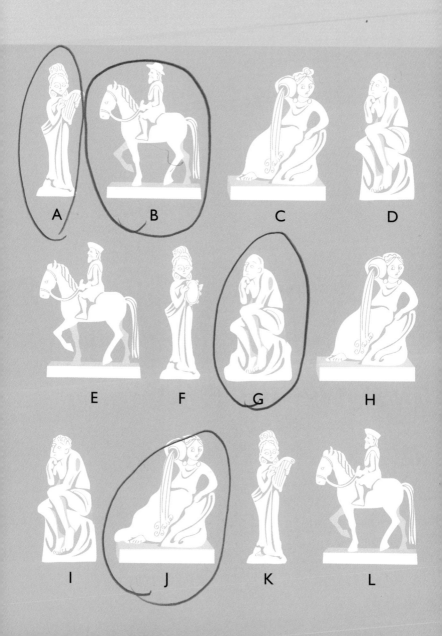

Sandcastle scores

Five children took part in a sandcastle building competition. The judges marked their castles out of 60. Use the clues to find out how many points the children got. Who won?

Callum scored 35% of the possible 60 points.
Ramona's sandcastle scored 54.
Kylie scored half as many points as Ramona.
Brian scored 12 fewer points than Kylie.
David scored $2/5$ of the possible points.

Callum ....   **Ramona** ....   **David** ....

Kylie ....   **Brian** ....

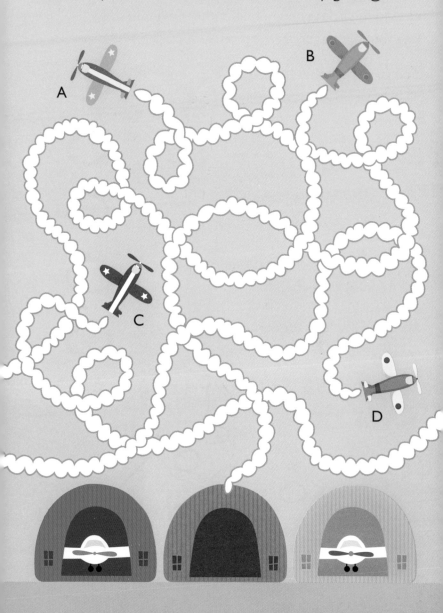

Plane trails

Circle the plane that has come from the empty hangar.

Busy month

Natalie has five activities planned for June and has circled their dates on her calendar. Can you draw a line to match each activity to the correct date?

She is going to her friend's sleepover on a Saturday night.

She has her first karate lesson on a Wednesday.

Her sister's birthday party is before the sleepover.

She is doing a sponsored walk in the middle of the month.

She is going to a concert exactly two weeks after the sleepover.

4

12

15

26

30

Left and right

In this picture, what is ...

1. ... two items to the left of the item that is three items to the right of the item that is three items to the right of the item that is two items to the left of the item that is immediately to the right of the clock?

Answer: Cheese

2. ... two items to the right of the item that is two items to the right of the item that is immediately to the left of the item that is four items to the right of the item that is immediately to the left of the teddy bear?

Answer: Rocket

Sheep and lambs

Each sheep should have two lambs. How many lambs are missing?

Answer: ....

Prove it!

In each set of statements below, underline the **two** that prove:

1. Ali is eating strawberry ice cream.

    a. Ali's ice cream is in a cone.

    b. Sonia is eating strawberry ice cream.

    c. Ali's ice cream has pieces of fruit in it.

    d. Sonia's ice cream has a cherry on top.

    e. Ali's ice cream is the same as Sonia's.

2. Suzi is a rock singer.

    a. Suzi's band only plays rock music.

    b. Singing rock music requires a strong voice.

    c. Suzi sings in a band.

    d. Suzi has a strong voice.

    e. Suzi loves rock music.

3. Marvin goes cycling every Sunday.

    a. Marvin knows how to cycle and rollerblade.

    b. Jane sometimes cycles with her little brother.

    c. Jane goes rollerblading every week.

    d. Jane goes cycling every Sunday.

    e. Marvin and Jane always go cycling together.

Text message code

A criminal gang uses a secret code for text messages.

To type the letter "a" you would normally press the 2 button once. Instead, the criminals press 3 once, typing the letter "d". Similarly, to type "h" you would normally press 4 twice. Instead, they press 5 twice, typing "k".

For any letters from the number 9 button, they use 2. So, instead of typing "w" by pressing 9 once, they type "a" by pressing 2 once.

For "s" and "z", they use 8 and 2, pressing them four times. So "s" becomes "8" and "z" becomes "2".

Can you decode the message shown on the right to help the police find the stolen goods?

Message: ....

....

....

....

Decipher this coded text message.

Mac McNab
April 01

02:30

Pdf, L klg wkh 8wrohq odtwrt8 lq pc ed8hphqw. 2df

1 . , '	2 ABC	3 DEF
4 GHI	5 JKL	6 MNO
7 PQRS	8 TUV	9 WXYZ

Pattern puzzle

Can you draw the next three patterns in the sequence?

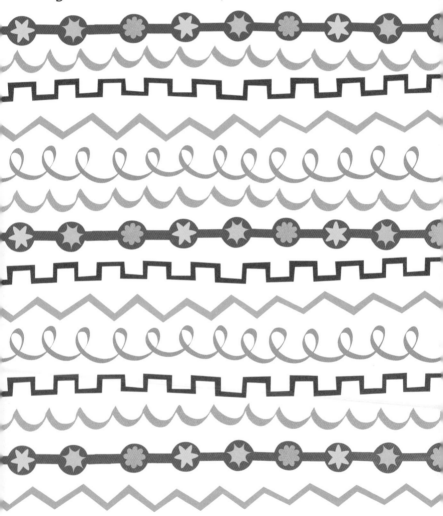

Hedge maze

Help this girl find her way through
the maze to reach the trophy
in the middle.

Addition grid

Write the black numbers below in the empty squares s
that each row and column adds up to the white numbe
next to it. You can only use each number once.

6   5   9   3   2

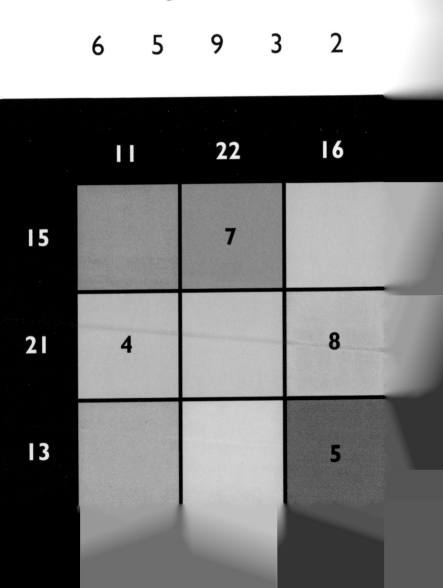

	11	22	16
15		7	
21	4		8
13			5

Lost list

Millie's shopping list fell out of her pocket before she reached the supermarket. Look at the list below for 30 seconds, then turn the page to see the things she bought. What did Millie forget?

Shopping list ...

Carrots
Peppers - I green, I red
Pineapple
Tomatoes
Banana
Lemon
Cauliflower
Bread
Cupcake
Apple
Cheese
Eggs

Lost list

Look at the previous page to see how to do this puzzle.

Answer: She didn't get bread

Xs in squares

Can you place six Xs in the grid below without making three-in-a-row in any direction?

Mummy's message

An ancient tomb has been discovered in Egypt with a message written in hieroglyphics on the wall. Use the code on the opposite page to see what it means.

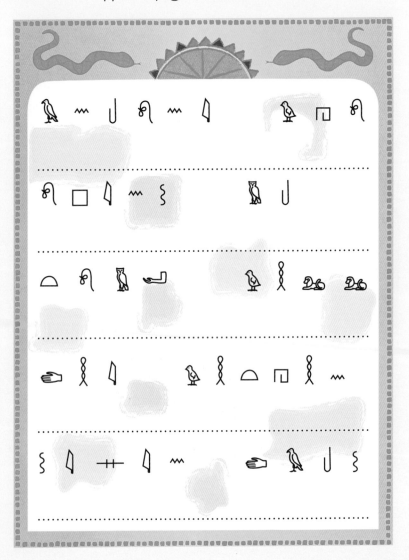

A — (vulture)
B — (leg/foot)
C — (reed shelter)
D — (hand)
E — (reed)
F — (horned viper)
G — (jar stand)
H — (twisted flax / house)
I — (reed)
J — (leg)
K — (basket)
L — (lion)
M — (owl)
N — (water)
O — (lasso)
P — (stool)
Q — (hill)
R — (mouth)
S — (folded cloth)
T — (loaf)
U — (quail chick)
V — (twist)
W — (quail chick)
X — (basket)
Y — (two reeds)
Z — (bolt)

Hippo hop

Can you draw a path across this jungle river, landing only on rocks, and avoiding the hippos?

Start

Finish

Waiter, waiter!

Memorize these orders for one minute, then turn the page and draw lines to connect the items with the correct tables.

Table 1

Fish and salad

Selection of cupcakes

Water

Table 2

Burger and fries

Ice cream sundae

Orange juice

Table 3

Ham sandwich

Grapes

Strawberry milkshake

Waiter, waiter!

Look at the previous page to find out how to do this puzzle.

Seeds and flowers

Joey, Lou, Alex, Dionne and Kelly planted 87 flower seeds. One month later, they counted how many of their seeds had grown into flowers.

Joey planted 16 seeds, and ¼ of them had grown.
Lou planted one seed less than Joey, and ⅓ of hers had grown.
Alex and Dionne each planted three more seeds than Lou.
⅓ of Alex's seeds had grown.
½ of Dionne's seeds had grown.
¼ of Kelly's seeds had grown.

What is the total number of flowers that had grown?

............of Joey's seeds had grown.

............of Lou's seeds had grown.

............of Alex's seeds had grown.

............of Dionne's seeds had grown.

............of Kelly's seeds had grown.

Answer:.....................................

Dragon spotting

Use the book below to find out which dragon is shown on the opposite page. Who should be afraid of it? Circle the correct answer:

the princess / the knights / the sheep / the villagers

> **Draco**

Mischievous, kidnaps princesses, breathes smoke.

< **Amfyre**

Breathes toxic gas, aggressive, fights knights.

> **Ringol**

Secretive, steals sheep, breathes fog.

< **Crizard**

Cruel, breathes jets of fire, burns down villages.

Odd one out

Circle the odd one out in each row.

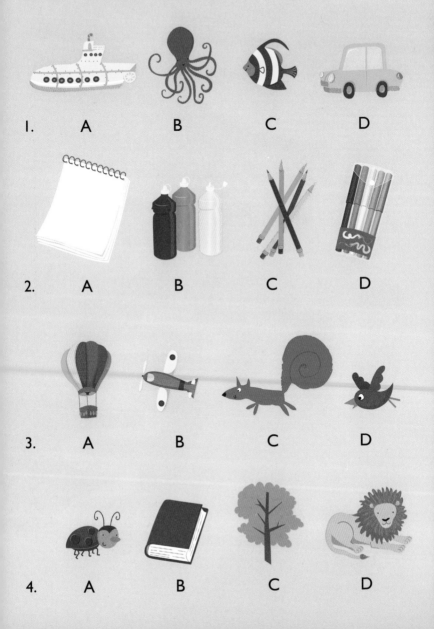

1. A B C D

2. A B C D

3. A B C D

4. A B C D

Jigsaw puzzle

Circle the two pieces that will finish this jigsaw puzzle.

True or false?

True or false? Put T or F in the circles. In this picture ...

1. ... there are nine yellow fish.

2. ... there are more striped fish than spotted fish.

3. ... there are more turtles than seahorses.

4. ... there are no jellyfish.

Top gamer

Three children each played two computer games. Using the information, calculate each player's combined score.

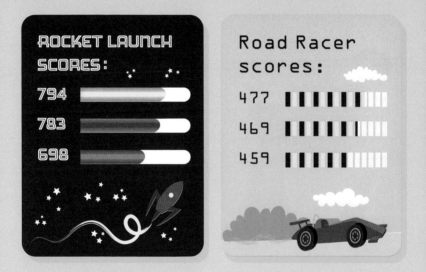

ROCKET LAUNCH SCORES:
794
783
698

Road Racer scores:
477
469
459

Ravi scored ten more than John on "Road Racer". Laura got the middle score on "Rocket Launch". John scored 239 points more on "Rocket Launch" than on "Road Racer".

Ravi's combined score:

John's combined score:

Laura's combined score:

Find me

Can you find these people in the scene on the opposite page? They're wearing the same clothes, but may not be in the same poses.

Happy endings

Draw a line to join each unfinished word to its ending.

decom...................

dist......................

templ....................

overti....................

spokes...................

relea.....................

journa...................

suit.......................

man

able

red

ate

ant

pose

sing

list

On the bus

Look at the passengers on these buses for 30 seconds, then turn the page and circle the extra passengers.

On the bus

Look at the previous page to find out how to do this puzzle.

Cooking confusion

These pictures from a recipe have become jumbled up.
Write the numbers in the order the pictures should appear.

1

2

3

4

5

6

7

8

Answer: ....

Sale on Saturn

The unit of currency on Saturn is the Jark, and there are 100 Yargons in one Jark. Something that costs five Jarks and 40 Yargons, for example, is written as J 5.40. Can you calculate the cost of the items?

a. The burger and drink costs:...

b. The anti-gravity boots cost:...

c. The toy spaceship costs:...

d. The freeze ray gun costs:...

e. The sunglasses cost:...

f. The cuddly space cat costs:...

g. The cuddly alien costs:...

h. The T-shirt costs:...

Opposites

Circle the two words in each line that have *opposite* meanings. For example:

(late)	long	last	even	(early)	end
back	towards	before	above	alone	after
long	large	lean	small	safe	sad
gain	give	great	take	tame	tall
alive	angry	able	dull	dark	dead
hot	happy	heavy	late	light	lost
pale	pretty	poor	rich	rare	right
fat	fast	faint	thin	thaw	open
shy	shut	shrink	good	grow	glue

Web letters

Can you find the nine-letter word hiding in the grid?
Move from one letter to another, using each letter
only once.

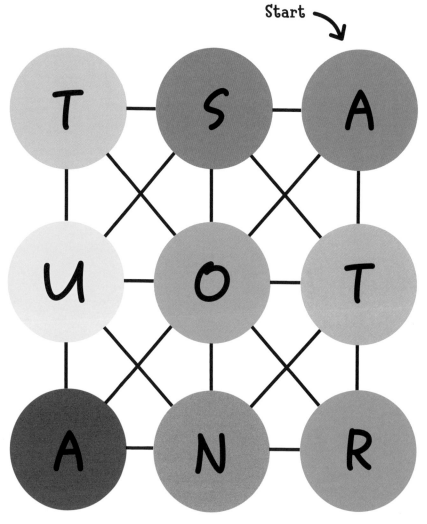

Dot-to-dot

Join the dots in alphabetical order to finish the picture.

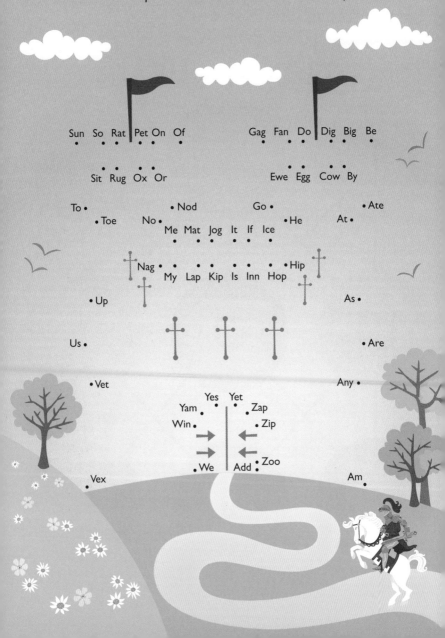

Sun So Rat Pet On Of   Gag Fan Do Dig Big Be

Sit Rug Ox Or   Ewe Egg Cow By

To   Nod   Go   Ate
   Toe   No   He   At
           Me Mat Jog It If Ice

      Nag   Hip
         My Lap Kip Is Inn Hop

   Up   As

Us   Are

   Vet   Any

            Yes Yet
      Yam   Zap
      Win   Zip

                        Zoo
            We   Add

   Vex   Am

Butterfly wings

Study this picture for one minute. Then, turn the page and see if you can fill in the correct squares to make a matching picture.

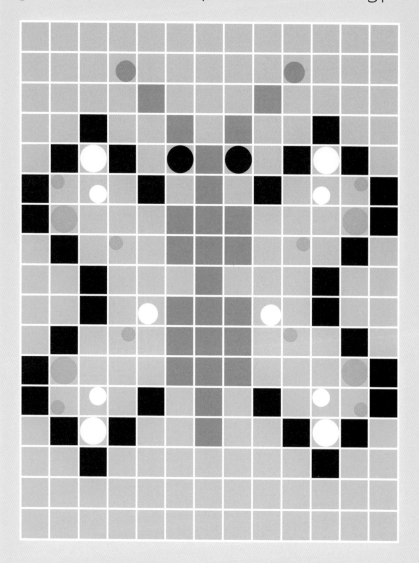

Butterfly wings

Look at the previous page for instructions on how to do this puzzle.

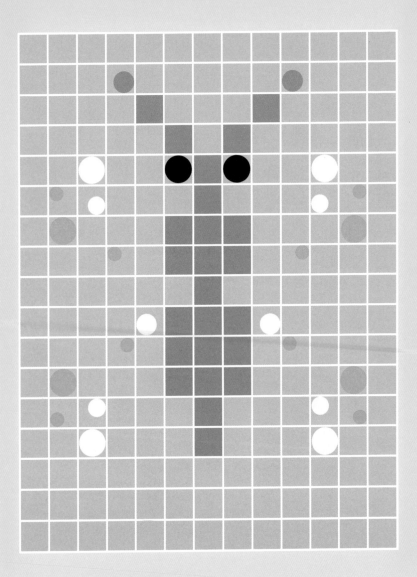

Find the fish

Look at these fish for one minute, then turn the page. Can you name the fish that is missing from the next page?

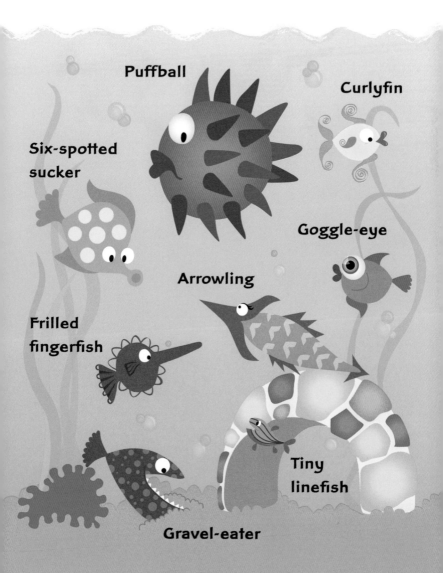

Puffball

Curlyfin

Six-spotted sucker

Goggle-eye

Arrowling

Frilled fingerfish

Tiny linefish

Gravel-eater

Find the fish

Look at the previous page to find out how to do this puzzle.

Answer: ....

Matching buttons

Circle the button that **isn't** one of a matching pair.

Creepy-crawly count

How many creepy-crawlies are there in this picture?

Answer: ....

What's the time?

1. A piece of string one hundred units long is wrapped around a spool. It takes one second to cut a unit length of the string. How many seconds will it take to cut one hundred unit lengths?

Answer: ....

2. Draw a straight line to split this clockface in half so that the sum of the numbers on one side of the line is equal to the sum of the numbers on the other side.

3. Following the sequence, what time should watch D show?

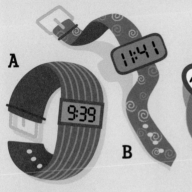

A **9:39**

B **11:41**

C **14:44**

D

Answer: ....

Chicken maze

Help this hen find her way to her chicks.

Picture pairs

The pictures below each have a matching picture on the next page. Look at this page for one minute and try to memorize the pictures and the numbers that go with them. Then, turn the page and write the correct numbers on the matching pictures.

Picture pairs

Look at the previous page to find out how to do this puzzle.

Alien birthday

In Alvin the Alien's language:

RAFF FISG PIRD means "Happy birthday, father."

PIRD GOL MYDAR RAFF means "Father is happy today."

WIRL GOL MYDAR RAFF means "Mother is happy today."

Can you draw a line to the word that means:

1. Father?

2. Mother?

3. Happy?

4. Birthday?

RAFF

WIRL

GOL

PIRD

FISG

MYDAR

RAFF FISG PIRD

Royal wedding cake

At her wedding, Princess Ariana wants a huge wedding cake with lots of tiers and pillars. The royal bakers have 33 pillars in all. Each tier of the cake should be standing on one less pillar than the tier below it. How many tiers will the cake have, if it uses all the pillars? You can draw the cake to help you find the answer. The first two tiers and sets of pillars have already been drawn.

Answer: ....

Missing symbols

Fill in the missing symbols to make each line true.
Use **<** (which means "is less than"), **>** (which means "is more than") or **=** (which means "is equal to").

a. 0.20	¼
b. 210 minutes	3½ hours
c. months in a year	days in two weeks
d. sides of a hexagon	sides of a pentagon
e. legs on a spider	tentacles on an octopus
f. zeros in one million	zeros in four million
g. years in six decades	years in half a century
h. hearts in a pack of cards	clubs in a pack of cards
i. faces on a pair of dice	faces on a cuboid
j. hands in a string quartet	heads in a soccer team

Treasure island

Using the map and directions, can you mark an X on the spot where the pirate treasure is hidden?

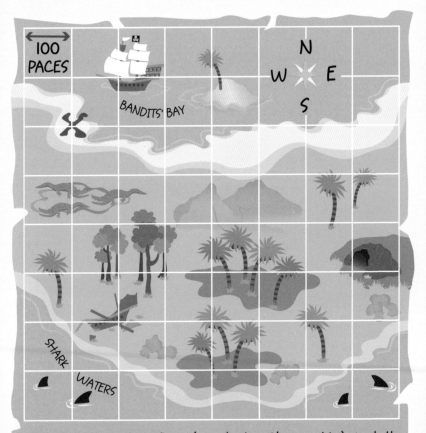

Begin at Bandits' Bay (marked with a red X). Walk 100 paces South and 500 paces East. Then 200 paces South and 100 paces East. In here, you'll find the key to the treasure chest. Then walk another 100 paces South. Finally, take 500 paces West, and you'll find the treasure chest in here.

I spy

Spend one minute memorizing the things Secret Agent Q has to do tomorrow and the times when he has to do them. Then, turn the page.

Pick up secret mission details and disguise from Headquarters.

Board flight to Catzberg.

Pick up top secret package from Agent X at the train station.

Drop off package at old factory in Romsky Forest.

AGENT Q

I spy

Study the previous page for one minute, then try to
answer the questions below **without looking back**.

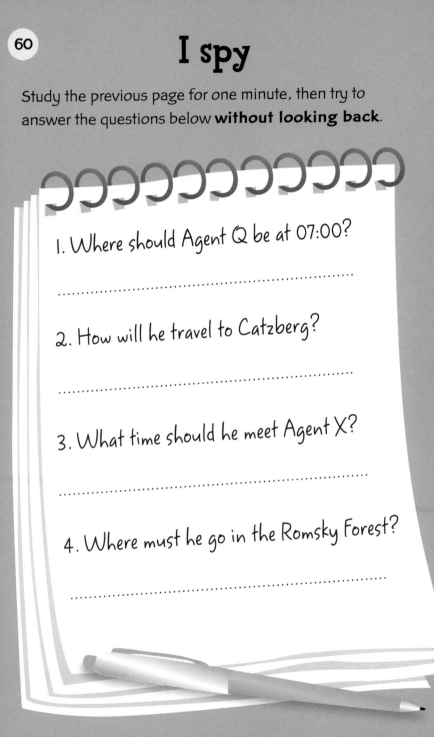

1. Where should Agent Q be at 07:00?

....

2. How will he travel to Catzberg?

....

3. What time should he meet Agent X?

....

4. Where must he go in the Romsky Forest?

....

Party hats

Look at these party hats for 30 seconds, then turn the page.

Party hats

Look at the party hats on the previous page for 30 seconds, then turn back and read the text below to find out what to do.

Can you remember which party hat pattern is missing from the ones above and draw it on the empty hat?

Out of place

There are **three** strange things in each of these pictures.
Can you find and circle them?

Relative riddles

See if you can solve these riddles.

Riddle 1: Mary's father has five daughters. The oldest four are named Nana, Nene, Nini and Nono. What's the name of the youngest daughter?

Riddle 2: Two fathers and two sons went fishing. By the end of the day each of them had caught two fish, but there were only six fish in the bucket. How could this be?

Riddle 3: A dying king wants to leave his kingdom to the wiser of his two sons. He tells them that he will hold a horse race, and the son whose horse finishes last will inherit the realm. The younger son immediately jumps on a horse and rides it over the finish line at top speed. The king leaves him the kingdom. Why?

Riddle 4: Daniel is twice as old as his brother, David. In five years' time, David will be the same age as Daniel is now. How old are the brothers now?

Going trekking

Circle the **six** things below that an explorer would need to take on a daytime trek across a hot, dusty desert.

Word pad

Find the words on the notepad below and draw around them as shown here:

pen   **note**   **word**
paper   **write**   **draw**

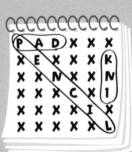

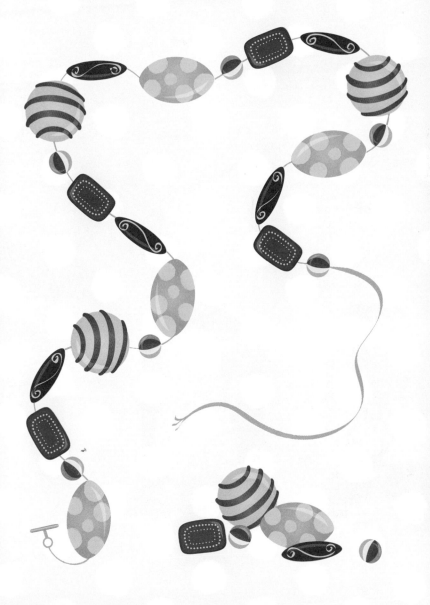

String of beads

Can you complete this necklace by drawing on three more beads in the correct order?

Out of time

Circle **six** things that wouldn't have been invented in Roman times.

Hungry caterpillars

Spot the caterpillars. If each one eats six leaves, how many leaves will be left on the branches?

Key chaos

Nine students have hung up their keys, but which set of keys belongs to whom? Write their initials on the labels.

Eli's keys are not on the bottom row.

Dawn's keys are on the left.

Fred's keys are directly above Bob's and next to Dawn's.

Isla's keys are on the right, on the row above Fred's.

Anna's keys are on the bottom row.

Claire's keys are directly above Fred's.

Greg's keys are directly above Harry's.

Petal puzzle

There are 13 flowers below, but only 12 single petals.
Can you circle the flower that has *no matching petal*?

Symbol search

In the pattern below, draw squares around the groups of symbols that match the groups shown on the right.

What's changed?

Look at this picture for one minute, then turn the page and circle the **six** objects that have moved or changed.

What's changed?

Look at the previous page to find out how to do this puzzle.

The way home

Hansel and Gretel are lost in the forest. They ask the forest creatures for directions.

The crow tells them:

"Go straight at the wishing well, then turn right. Once you're over the bridge, bear right, go past the rabbit holes, then turn left. Turn right, and you'll reach home."

The fox says:

"The crow's wrong. You have to turn left at the wishing well. Once you've passed the butterfly bush, turn right, then left. Then bear right, following the road over the bridge to reach home."

The weasel says:

"The others are wrong. You should go straight at the wishing well, then turn left. Take the second left, then turn right to reach home."

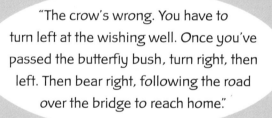

Turn the page to follow the routes, then circle the animal that gave them the correct directions.

The way home

Look at the previous page to find out how to do this puzzle.

Going dotty

Shade in the shapes with *orange* dots. What can you see?

Speech bubbles

All but one of these words can be paired with another one that has the opposite meaning. Find the odd one out, then write its opposite in the empty speech bubble to complete the set.

Picture pairs

The pictures below each have a matching picture on the next page. Look at this page for one minute and try to memorize the pictures and the numbers that go with them. Then, turn the page and write the correct numbers on the matching pictures.

Picture pairs

Look at the previous page to find out how to do this puzzle.

Web letters

Can you find the nine-letter word hiding in the grid? Move from one letter to another, using each letter only once.

Start

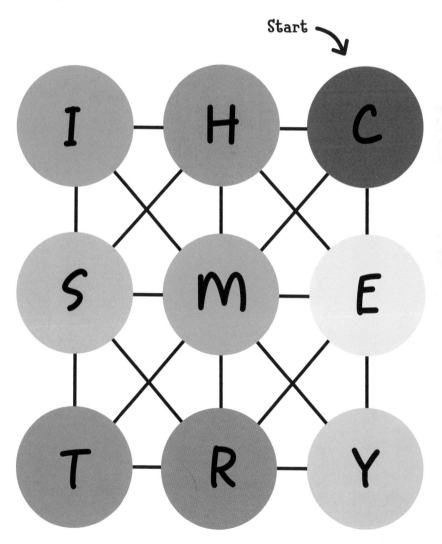

Fruit search

Find the names of the fruit in the grid and draw around them like this:

T	X	X	X	X	X	X
O	X	L	L	X	L	X
C	X	X	I	E	E	X
I	X	X	X	M	X	A
R	X	X	X	O	X	E
P	X	X	X	N	X	X
A	X	X	X	X	X	X

Apple   **Banana**   **Cherry**
Peach   **Orange**   **Pear**

N	A	N	A	N	A	B
A	E	P	P	A	Y	A
N	G	A	P	N	R	N
Y	N	E	E	L	R	Y
G	A	O	A	P	E	C
R	R	H	C	L	H	P
O	O	Y	H	A	C	A
C	T	C	L	P	N	Y

Matching bugs

Circle the two bugs that are a matching pair.

Missing symbols

Fill in the missing symbols to make each line true.
Use **<** (which means "is less than"), **>** (which means
"is more than") or **=** (which means "is equal to").

a.	The number of degrees in a circle	The number of days in a year
b.	The number of spots on a dice	The number of days in three week
c.	The number of planets in our solar system	The number of seas there are said to be
d.	The weight of a blue whale	The weight of ten elephants
e.	The distance from Earth to Jupiter	The distance from Earth to Saturn
f.	The number of wheels on a unicycle	The number of faces on a sphere
g.	The number of penguins in the Arctic	The number of lions in Africa
h.	The number of weeks in a year	The number of playing cards in a pack
i.	The freezing point of water	The freezing point of sea water

Key match-up

Circle the two pictures of keys that can be turned so that they match each other exactly.

Circle the two pictures of keys that can be turned so that they match each other exactly.

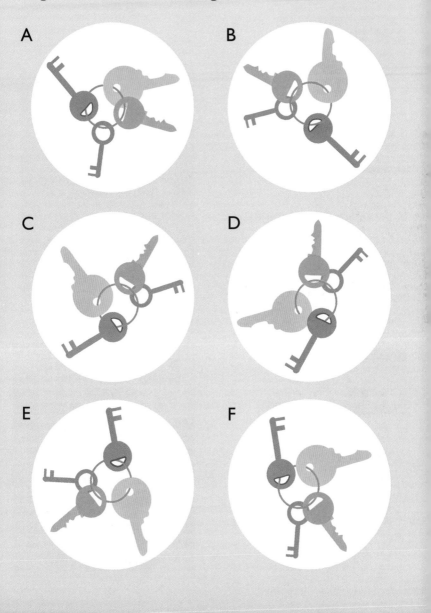

A

B

C

D

E

F

Answers

1. Pencil match-up
D and E

2. At the zoo
1. two
2. balloons
3. carrots
4. one
5. an ice cream

3. Monkey meals
B

4. Bees and butterflies
red: Flutter
orange: Buzzy
blue: Bizzy
purple: Flitter

5. Picture memory

6. Country search

7. Folding up
A, B, D and H

8. Planet paths

9. Patches

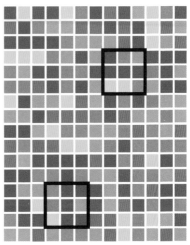

Answers

10. Puppy prize-giving

11. On and off

Two. He has to turn one light switch on for thirty seconds or so, then turn it off. Then, he should turn another switch on, go into the room and feel the lightbulbs. The bulb that's still warm is connected to the switch that he turned on first. The second switch he turned on controls the bulb that's lit, and the last bulb is connected to the switch that he didn't touch.

12. Empty pyramid

33 (It is 4 x 6 + 9).

13. Traffic jam

A9   B8   C6   D11   E12
F14   G10   H2   I1   J15
K4   L5   M3   N7   O13

14. Spot the difference

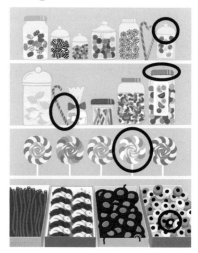

15. Going dotty

16. Twin chains

C and E

Answers

17. Spell check

This book is about a <u>dinosuar</u> who is afriad of <u>evrything</u>, even his own <u>refletion</u>. His dad is <u>embarrased</u> by him and he <u>does'nt</u> have any <u>freinds</u> because he is <u>two</u> boring to play with. One day, he <u>meats</u> a mouse who is brave, even <u>thuogh</u> he is little. The mouse teaches <u>Toomy</u> how to be brave <u>to</u>. I liked this book a lot <u>becuase</u> it was <u>funy</u>.

18. On the move

1. An hour and 20 minutes is the same as 80 minutes.
2. A cloud
3. Friday is the name of his horse.
4. It's daytime.

19. Statues

1.A   2.L   3.H   4.D

20. Sandcastle scores

Callum: 4th
Ramona: 1st
Kylie: 2nd
Brian: 5th
David: 3rd

21. Plane trails

A

22. Busy month

Sleepover: 12th
Karate: 30th
Party: 4th
Walk: 15th
Concert: 26th

23. Left and right

1. cheese
2. rocket

24. Sheep and lambs

4

25. Prove it!

1. b and e
2. a and c
3. d and e

26. Text message code

Mac, I hid the stolen laptops in my basement. Zac

27. Pattern puzzle

Answers

28. Hedge maze

29. Addition grid

	11	22	16
15	5	7	3
21	4	9	8
13	2	6	5

30. Lost list
Bread

31. Xs in squares
There are a few ways to do this puzzle. Here's one:

32. Mummy's message
ANYONE WHO OPENS
MY TOMB WILL DIE
WITHIN SEVEN DAYS

33. Hippo hop

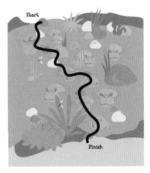

34. Waiter, waiter!

35. Seeds and flowers
29

36. Dragon spotting
the princess

Answers

37. Odd one out
1.D   2.A   3.C   4.B

38. Jigsaw puzzle
A and D

39. True or false?
1. True 3. False
2. True 4. False

40. Top gamer
Ravi : 1263

John : 1157

Laura : 1260

41. Find me

42. Happy endings
decompose

distant

template

overtired

spokesman

releasing

journalist

suitable

43. On the bus

44. Cooking confusion
7 8 1 2 5 6 3 4

45. Sale on Saturn
a. J 1.80   b. J 34.20

c. J 8.00   d. J 66.00

e. J 5.00   f. J 9.09

g. J 12.30   h. J 14.44

Answers

F

46. Opposites
before/after
large/small
give/take
alive/dead
heavy/light
poor/rich
fat/thin
shrink/grow

47. Web letters
ASTRONAUT

48. Dot-to-dot

49. Butterfly wings

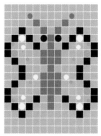

50. Find the fish
Goggle-eye

51. Matching buttons

52. Creepy-crawly count
34

53. What's the time?
1. 99 seconds 2.
3. 18:48

54. Chicken maze

55. Picture pairs

Answers

56. Alien birthday
1. PIRD 2. WIRL 3. RAFF 4. FISG

57. Royal wedding cake
7 tiers

58. Missing symbols
a.< b.= c.< d.> e.=
f.= g.> h.= i.> j.<

59. Treasure island
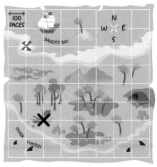

60. I spy
Headquarters, plane,
2:00 p.m., old factory

61. Party hats

62. Out of place

63. Relative riddles
1. Mary
2. One of the three men is
both a father and a son.
3. The younger son rode
his brother's horse over
the line.
4. Daniel is 10; David is 5.

64. Going trekking

Answers

65. Word pad

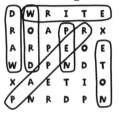

66. String of beads

67. Out of time

68. Hungry caterpillars

8

69. Key chaos

E	C	I
D	F	G
A	B	H

70. Petal puzzle

71. Symbol search

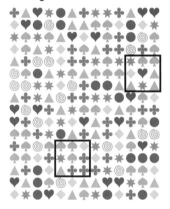

72. What's changed?

73. The way home

Answers

74. Going dotty

75. Speech bubbles

deep

76. Picture pairs

77. Web letters

CHEMISTRY

78. Fruit search

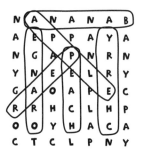

79. Matching bugs

80. Missing symbols

a. **<** b. **=** c. **>** d. **>** e. **<**

f. **=** g. **<** h. **=** i. **>**

81. Key match-up

C and F

Written by Sarah Khan. Designed by Joanne Kirkby. Illustrated by Lizzie Barber, Non Figg and Stella Baggott.

First published in 2014 by Usborne Publishing Ltd. 83–85 Saffron Hill, London ECIN 8RT, England. Copyright ©2014 Usborne Publishing Ltd. The name Usborne and the devices ♀ ⊕ are Trade Marks of Usborne Publishing Ltd. All rights reserved. No part of this publication may be reproduced, stored in a retrieval system, or transmitted in any form or by any means, electronic, mechanical, photocopying, recording or otherwise, without the prior permission of the publisher. UE.